volume

2

THE LEGEND OF
DORORO AND HYAKKIMARU

Created by
OSAMU TEZUKA

Adaptation by
SATOSHI SHIKI

CONTENTS

The Legend of the Hoofbeats in the Fog

PFFT...
HEH HEH HEH!

WHAT DO WE HAVE HERE... JUST A KID?
WHAT'S WITH YOU?!

WHAT A CREEP.
YOU SHOW UP OUTTA NOWHERE AND BURST INTO LAUGHTER WHEN YOU SEE MY FACE?
YOU DON'T LOOK ANY OLDER THAN A KID YOURSELF!

YOU'VE A SHARP TONGUE FOR ONE WITH SUCH A PRETTY FACE.
PRETTY ?!

IF YOU'RE MOIST-ENING A TOWEL...
IS SOMEONE ILL?

HMPH!
I DON'T KNOW YOU. IT'S NONE OF YOUR BEES-WAX.
FAIR POINT.

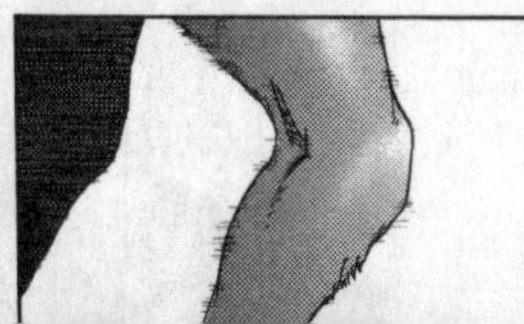

HEY!
WHY ARE YOU FOLLOWING ME?!
HEH HEH...

DON'T MIND ME.
GO ON, KEEP WALKING.

TCH!
IF I DIDN'T HAVE TO CARRY THIS WASHTUB, I'D SHAKE YOU OFF IN NO TIME FLAT.
HEH HEH HEH!

UNNGH...

!!
AAAAAAAHH!

BRO!
ARRRGH!

AHHHGH!
HEY, BRO!
ARE YOU OKAY? DOES IT HURT?

YOUR BROTHER?

......
NOT A REAL ONE.

IS HE SICK, OR INJURED?

WHICHEVER IT IS, HE CLEARLY ISN'T WELL.
GRRRGH...

URRGH...
IT'S NEITHER.

IT'S... HIS **EYES.**
I GUESS... THEY'RE **COMING BACK** RIGHT NOW...
AND HE'S IN PAIN...

JUST WHAT DOES THAT MEAN?
LOOK, I DON'T REALLY GET IT EITHER...
WAIT A SEC, WHY AM I TELLING **YOU** ANYTHING, ANYWAY?!

FORGET ABOUT IT!
HURRY UP AND GET LOST, WILL YA?!
HEH HEH!

IF YOU NEED ANYTHING, CALL ON ME AT MY RESIDENCE.
BWRRRR

ASK FOR THE HOUSE OF DAIGO. ANYONE IN THE AREA WILL KNOW THE NAME.
I AM CALLED TAHOMARU.

WHATEVER! WE DON'T NEED ANY HELP!
HEH HEH!

BRO...
ARE YOU OKAY?

YIKES!!
I CAN SEE...
DORORO...
HUH?

IT'S BLURRY... BUT I CAN SEE.
SO THAT'S YOUR FACE.

YOU CAN SEE MY FACE...?
DOES THAT MEAN...
ALL THIS TIME, YOU COULDN'T...?
......
IS VISION REALLY THIS DIZZYING?

SO THAT'S WHAT YOU LOOK LIKE, DORORO.
YOU'RE SURPRIS-INGLY CUTE.
AW, SHUCKS!
YOU'RE MAKIN' ME BLUSH, BRO!
I EXPECTED YOU TO LOOK MORE BOYISH.
SAY WHAT?!

WH-WHAT THE HECK ARE YOU SAYING?!

HEY... BRO...
DON'T YOU THINK IT'S TIME YOU TOLD ME A FEW THINGS?

I WANT TO HEAR YOUR STORY.

TAHOMARU. YOU WERE SAFE?

FATHER.

MY BLOOD RAN COLD WHEN I LOST SIGHT OF YOU IN THIS FOG. I THOUGHT YOU'D FALLEN INTO THE LAKE.
HEH HEH! YOU HAVE TOO LITTLE FAITH IN ME, FATHER.

WHAT IS IT?
NOTHING OF IMPORT.
I WAS MERELY RECALLING...

SOMEONE I MET...
THANKS TO THIS FOG.

どろろと
百鬼丸伝

THE LEGEND OF
DORORO AND HYAKKIMARU

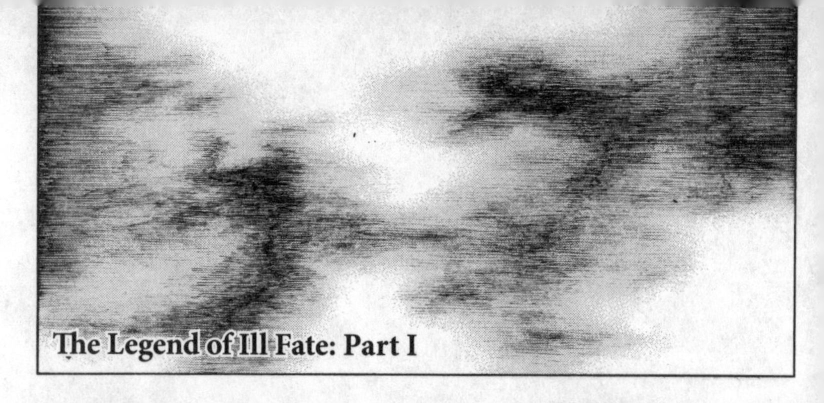

The Legend of Ill Fate: Part I

SHWRRRRRR

HEE HEE HEE HEE HEE!
SHWRRRRRR
SHWRL
WELL...
SEEMS I'M CONCERNED ABOUT HYAKKI-MARU AFTER ALL...
DEAR ME...

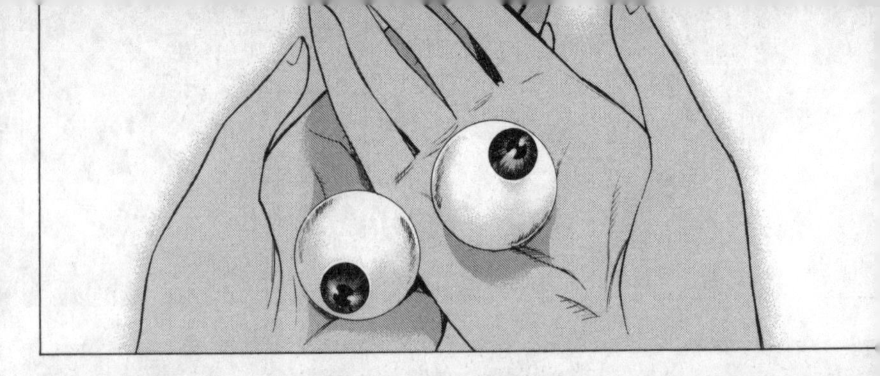

DORORO.
THOSE EYEBALLS ARE...

I KNOW. THEY'RE **GLASS EYES,** RIGHT?

MY EARS, TOO.

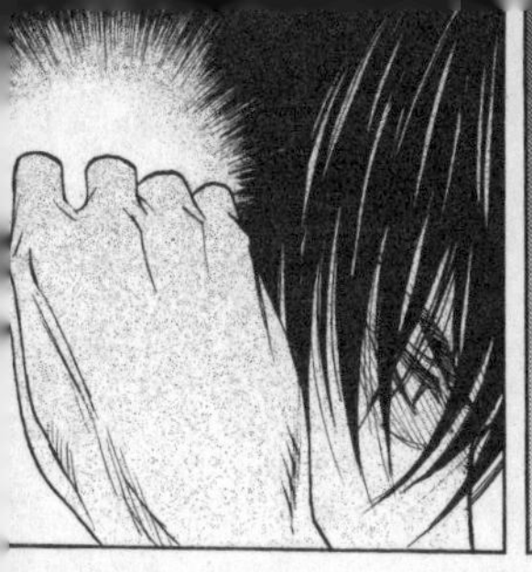

THEY'RE FAKE.

I CAN'T ACTUALLY HEAR A WORD YOU SAY.
I FEEL THE VIBRATIONS IN THE AIR, AND MY ENTIRE BODY KNOWS WHAT YOU'RE SAYING. SO IT'S ESSENTIALLY THE SAME AS IF I HAD EARS.
GULP

SCARED?

I WOULDN'T BLAME YOU IF YOU WERE.

SO THIS IS MY STORY...

I'M TOLD THAT WHEN I WAS A BABY...
I CAME DRIFTING DOWN A RIVER IN A WASHTUB.

SNARL
GRRRR
SHOO! SHOO!!
GET LOST, YOU MANGY STRAYS!!
DID A BODY WASH UP?
SPLISH
A WASH-TUB?

THE MAN WHO FOUND MY WASHTUB...
WAS A PEASANT WHO LIVED NEARBY.

WHOA!!
HRRRRM...
HMPH...
WHATSA-MATTA HIBUKURO? WHY THE SCOWL?
ITACHI...
AHA! I BET YOU FOUND SOME FOOD YOU DON'T WANNA SHARE!
LET ME SEE!

YEEK!
WH... WHAT IS THAT THING...?
A... A BABY?
IT CAN'T BE...
I MEAN, IT...
IT DOESN'T HAVE ARMS OR LEGS...OR A NOSE... OR EVEN **EYES!**
WHERE ARE YOU GOIN'?
IF IT'S A BABY, IT NEEDS A **TEAT.**

EH?! DON'T TELL ME YOU'RE TAKIN' IT TO *HER*...?
I DON'T THINK THAT'S SUCH A GOOD IDEA!
SHE ONLY LOST HER BABY--
THAT'S WHY I'M GONNA DO IT.
GOTTA GIVE THIS POOR THING SOME MILK, AT ANY RATE.
DARLING... WHAT HAPPENED TO HIM...?!
NO CLUE...
ALL I KNOW IS IT DRIFTED DOWN THE RIVER IN A WASH-TUB...

TWITCH
TWITCH
IT'S BEEN LIKE THAT SINCE I FOUND IT.
IT DOESN'T HAVE ANY-THING...
NO EYES, NO EARS... NO ARMS OR LEGS...
GIVEN HOW IT HASN'T CRIED, MAYBE IT DOESN'T HAVE A **VOICE** EITHER...
BUT THAT BABY'S **ALIVE**...
SLIP...
SO PLEASE, OJIYA...
I KNOW YOU'RE HURTING SO SOON AFTER WE LOST OUR KID, BUT WILL YA--
RUSTLe

SUCK
HE LATCHED!!
FOR GOODNESS' SAKE...
DAY-TO-DAY SURVIVAL IS HARD ENOUGH AS IT IS WITH THESE WARS. WHY WOULD YOU ADD ANOTHER MOUTH TO FEED?

BUT, DEAR...
HOW WILL WE RAISE HIM?
HE CAN NURSE...
BUT WHAT ABOUT THE FUTURE...?
I'M THINKIN' I'LL TAKE 'IM...
TO THE DOC. TO **JUKAI-SENSEI.**

THE PEASANT WHO FOUND ME THEN TOOK ME...
TO A DOCTOR OF GREAT SKILL AND SCHOLARSHIP BY THE NAME OF **JUKAI.**

HRRM...

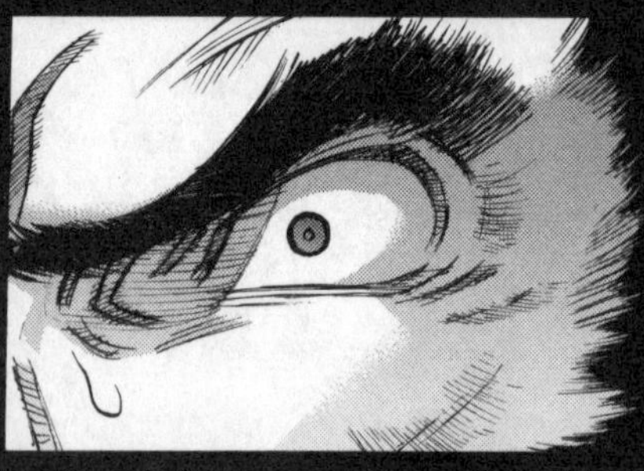

TWITCH
TWITCH

MY WORD...!

WH... WHAT DO YOU THINK, DOC...?
WILL HE GET BETTER?

IT'S NOT SO SIMPLE AS THAT.
HOW DID THIS HAPPEN...?
THIS BABY HAS NOTHING.
NO EYES, NO EARS, NO NOSE...NO ARMS OR LEGS...
NOT EVEN A VOICE.
PERHAPS NOT EVEN EMOTIONS...
B-BUT, DOC, HE'S ALIVE, AIN'T HE?!
WELL, YES...
......
THIS PLACE IS HELL ON EARTH...

TO BE BORN HERE LIKE THIS... WHAT A TERRIBLE FATE...
WHO ABANDONED IT? AN ONI? OR A YOKAI? OR...
RUSTLE...

ALL RIGHT.
LET'S ALL RAISE THIS CHILD, TOGETHER!!

BECAUSE OF MY CONDITION, THEY DECIDED I'D BE RAISED AT JUKAI'S HOME...
AND THE HUSBAND AND WIFE WOULD PROVIDE ME WITH MILK.

GOTTA THANK 'EM BOTH FOR THAT!

......
SEASONS PASSED...

WINTERS...
SPRINGS...
SUMMERS...
AND AUTUMNS...

THE DOCTOR MADE MY BODY WITH HIS OWN HANDS.

GEE...

SO... HE MADE THESE ARMS...

I...
MOVED MY NEW ARMS AND LEGS, AND STUMBLING...
I WALKED.
JUST MOVING SENT PAIN SHOOTING THROUGH ME...
PAIN SO GREAT I THOUGHT I WOULD FAINT...
DAY...
AFTER DAY...
I FOUGHT THE PAIN.
AND IN TIME...

EVERY FEW YEARS, THE DOCTOR MADE ME A NEW BODY IN PACE WITH MY GROWTH.

WHAT ABOUT THE COUPLE WHO FOUND YOU?

I'VE HEARD THEY COULDN'T MAKE THE TRIP ANYMORE...
BECAUSE OF A WALL BUILT BETWEEN THE DOCTOR'S HOME AND THEIRS, CALLED BANMON.

JUKAI TOLD ME HE DOESN'T KNOW WHAT BECAME OF THEM AFTERWARD EITHER.
THWACK

THWACK

I KNOW I MADE THAT BODY FOR HIM...
BUT I NEVER DREAMED HE'D BE ABLE TO MOVE IT SO FREELY...

THE BOY MUST HAVE A POWER UNFATHOMABLE TO US ORDINARY PEOPLE.

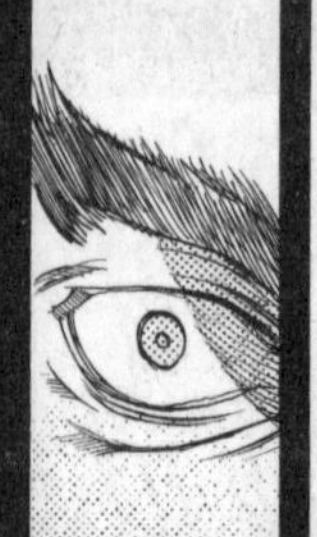

POWER...?
UNKNOWN...
POWER...?!
IS IT SOMETHING HE HONED DUE TO HIS CONDITION...?
OR SOMETHING HE HAD ALL ALONG, FROM BIRTH...?
THOK

A POWER THAT EXCEEDS HUMAN CAPABILITIES...

NO, WHAT AM I THINKING?!
IT'S POINTLESS TO PONDER IT WHEN I KNOW NONE OF THE FACTS.

SOMETHING'S THE MATTER WITH ME.
GOOD! IT'S MY TURN!
MY SON IS HUMAN. A PERFECTLY UNREMARKABLE HUMAN.

FOUND YOU...

ONE DAY...
WITHOUT WARNING...A DEMON BECAME AWARE OF MY EXISTENCE.

HE TURNED OUR LIFE UPSIDE DOWN.

SON, I'VE FINISHED SEEING PATIENTS FOR THE DAY.
DRAW A BATH FOR ME, WOULD YOU?

どろろと
百鬼丸伝

THE LEGEND OF DORORO AND HYAKKIMARU

RUSTLE
RUSTLE
RUSTLE
RUSTLE
The Legend of Ill Fate: Part II
RUSTLE
RUSTLE
RUSTLE
SO... YOU WERE STILL ALIVE, WERE YOU?
WHAT IS THAT VESSEL?

WHY, IT'S ALMOST AS THOUGH...

YOU FANCY YOURSELF HUMAN.

KA-KRAK

TO THINK YOU SURVIVED IN **THAT STATE...**
OH, THAT FATEFUL DAY...
CRACKLE
CRACKLE

WE OUGHT TO HAVE SHREDDED THE SCRAPS-- WHAT LITTLE REMAINED OF YOU-- TOO...
FWOOSH
ROOOAAAR
HWOOOO
BE A GOOD LITTLE BOY AND KEEP STILL.
I'LL TEAR YOU APART WHERE YOU STA--
SHUNK

AH!
GAH!
GYAAAH!
!
GRAB

RUN, SON!!
ROAAAR

CRUNCH

SHWOOOO
OOOOOO
CRUNCH

SHWOOOO

GLORP

......
YOU
...

※Abe no Seimei was a legendary diviner and spiritualist of the imperial court during the Heian period, sometimes called the "Merlin of Japan."

WHY, YOU...!
I'LL NEED YOU DEMONS TO MAKE YOURSELVES SCARCE FOR A LITTLE WHILE.

THAT SAID, I'VE DIED ONCE, TOO...
METHINKS I MAY BE A LITTLE RUSTY--

SHAAAAA
WHEW...

THE PATHS WERE BLOCKED BY LANDSLIDES AND MORE EVERYWHERE WE WENT...
BUT NOW THAT WE'VE TAKEN SHELTER, WE CAN FINALLY RELAX.
RIGHT, SON?

STILL, WHAT A SHOCK!

FIRST TIME I'VE EVER HAD A PATIENT OF **THAT** SORT!
I SUPPOSE EVEN EVIL SPIRITS GO TO THE DOCTOR WHEN THEY FALL ILL! I'LL BE DAMNED!
WHERE IN THE WORLD DID THAT MONSTER GET WIND OF MY REPUTATION AS A GENIUS DOCTOR?
BWA HA HA HA!
WHAP

I KNOW FULL WELL...
THEY DIDN'T COME FOR ME.
IT'S MY SON THEY WANT.

THOSE THINGS ARE AFTER...
THE MYSTERIOUS POWER THAT DWELLS WITHIN MY BOY.
PLIP
SON...
TELL ME SOMETHING.
THE "FATEFUL DAY" OF WHICH THAT EVIL SPIRIT SPOKE...
DO YOU REMEMBER ANYTHING OF IT?
IF THERE'S ANYTHING AT ALL YOU REMEMBER, PLEASE TELL ME.

あ
yes
I SEE...

IS THAT... A FACE?
A SCAR...?

THIS SCAR ON THE FOREHEAD...
IT ALMOST LOOKS LIKE DAIGO-SAMA, THE MAN WHO ROSE AS A VASSAL OF THE TOGASHI CLAN...

?!!
BWOOMF

SON!!
BOOOM
!!
GAH ...!
ROAAAAR
YOU WON'T ES-CAPE ME...

ROOOA
AAAAR

!!

BAH!

AHHH...
IT HURTS ...!
IT HURTS ...

WHOOM

!!
BOOM

ROAAAR

ONLY A SWORD ENCHANTED BY HIM SHOULD BE CAPABLE OF WOUNDING US.
COULD THAT SWORD BE...?

I RECEIVED THIS SWORD AS A GIFT FROM A GENERAL WHEN I WAS YOUNG...

I BELIEVE HE SAID HE'D HAD IT ENCHANTED BY A CERTAIN MONK...

LISTEN WELL!

BOY WITH-
OUT A
NAME!

?!
WH- WHO'S THERE ?!
ASK NOT.
YOU NEED BUT LISTEN.
IT...
CAN-NOT...
BE...

CHILD.
YOU ARE MISSING FORTY-EIGHT PIECES OF YOURSELF.
THEY WERE TAKEN FROM YOU BY DEMONS...
LIKE THE ONE OVER THERE.
I SEE... THIS PLACE...

SEIMEI!!
IS THIS YOUR GRAVE?!!
GAH! YOU BAITED ME!
YOU LURED ME HERE!! WHAT NERVE!!
KRUK
BA-
BWOK

GA-
BOOOSH
CLENCH
I CANNOT... MOVE...!
UGH...!
BWOK
BWOK

BWOK
SHLUP
SHLUP
!!
FIGHT THEM. FIGHT YOUR FORTY-SEVEN DEMONS AND ONE DEMON GOD.
IF YOU CAN DEFEAT THEM...
THEN, MY BOY...

YOU MIGHT BE ABLE TO BECOME **HUMAN** AGAIN.
I...
I CAN'T BE-LIEVE THIS!
IT'S TOO DANGER-OUS...
AH!
....

YOU MUST BE THE ONE TO SLAY THE DEMONS.
AH...

IT WON'T MEAN ANYTHING UNLESS YOU DEFEAT THEM.

I SLEW THE FIRST DEMON JUST LIKE THAT SAGE TOLD ME...
AND THE PIECE OF MYSELF I RECLAIMED FROM IT WAS MY **VOICE.**

JUKAI'S SWORD... IT WAS A SWORD THAT SAGE HAD ONCE IMBUED WITH SPIRIT ENERGY.

I MADE UP MY MIND TO LEAVE JUKAI AND SET OUT ON MY OWN.

HE'D RAISED ME AS HIS OWN SON. HE DIDN'T APPROVE...
BUT AS LONG AS HE WAS WITH ME...
DEMONS MIGHT ATTACK US AGAIN AT ANY TIME.

I DIDN'T WANT TO PUT MY POPS IN DANGER... SO I HAD TO DO IT.

AFTER I MADE MY DECISION, JUKAI GAVE ME MY NAME-- **HYAKKI-MARU.**

AFTER THAT...

OVER THE COURSE OF A YEAR, JUKAI MADE ME A NEW BODY.
A BODY THAT COULD STAND UP TO THOSE DEMONS.
HE GAVE ME THE BLADES IN MY ARMS AND THE WEAPONS CONCEALED THROUGHOUT MY BODY, ALL SO I COULD RECLAIM MYSELF.
IN THE MEANTIME, THAT SAGE TAUGHT ME HOW TO USE MY SUPER-NATURAL--

WAAAAAH!

UNGH... I HAD NO IDEA YOU HAD SUCH A SAD PAST... THAT YOU'D BEEN FIGHTING ALL BY YOUR LONESOME UP UNTIL NOW!
YOU AREN'T ALONE ANYMORE! YOU'VE GOT ME WITH YOU FROM NOW ON!
DON'T CRY, BRO!

YOU'RE THE ONE CRYING, WEIRDO.

......
EH HEH HEH HEH...

OH YEAH...
WHAT'S TAKING THE OLD LUTE-TOTING MONK SO LONG?

YEESH! HOW FAR DID HE GO TO GET MEDICINAL HERBS?

OH!

MONK!

WHY'D YOU COME BACK WITH-OUT ANY HERBS?!

ECH! YOU'RE FILTHY! WHAT HAPPENED TO YOU?
HYEE HEE...
OH, I TOOK A LITTLE SPILL... S'POSE I WAS A MITE KNACKERED.

ARGH! IF YOU'RE TIRED, THEN YOU OUGHTA REST!
SPLISH

タッ
TUMP
タッ
TUMP

HERE, AT LEAST WIPE YOUR FACE!
YOU'RE HOPELESS.

SHFF

HWOOOOOOO
PA...MY ELBOWS HURT...
SHH!

WE'RE ALMOST PAST **BANMON.**
IF WE CAN JUST CROSS IT, WE'LL BE IN ASAKURA TERRITORY!
WE HAVE RELATIVES WE HAVEN'T SEEN IN YEARS AND YEARS OVER THERE. WE'LL GO TO THEM AND...

THOK
?!

THOK
THOK
THOK
THOK
KOME!
HEITA!!
THUNK

THUD
BANMON WAS A GIFT TO ME FROM FATHER.
I CANNOT ALLOW ANYONE THROUGH, NO MATTER WHO THEY ARE.

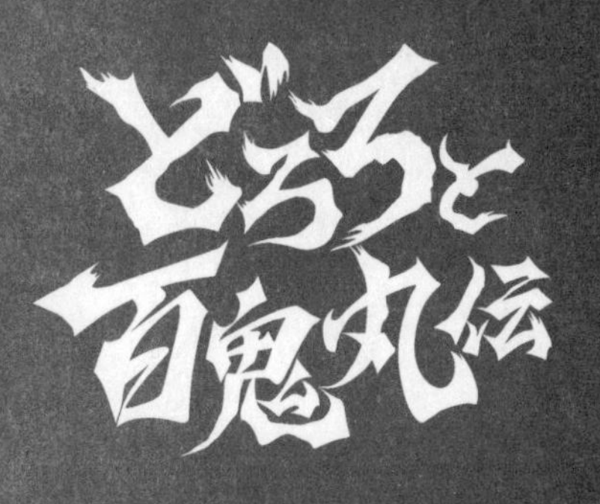
どろろと
百鬼丸伝

THE LEGEND OF
DORORO AND HYAKKIMARU

The Legend of Banmon: Part I

CRUNCH
CRUNCH

CRUNCH

SHAAAAAA

I CANNOT PERMIT ANY ATTEMPTS TO CROSS BANMON. NO EXCEPTIONS.

NOT EVEN FOR CHILDREN.

THUNK

I DID IT!
I GOT HIM!
I KILLED DAIGO KAGEMITSU'S SON, TAHOMARU!

HA HA HA HA HA!
CONTROL OF BANMON IS AS GOOD AS OURS NOW! GLORY TO THE ASAKURA ARMY!!
HA HA...
HA...?
SHRIK

CLACK
!!
HALF OF MY BODY...
WAS SACRIFICED FOR MY FATHER'S AMBITIONS.

THERE-FORE...
EEP ...!
GRRRK
THAT HALF OF MY BODY...
DOES NOT FEEL...

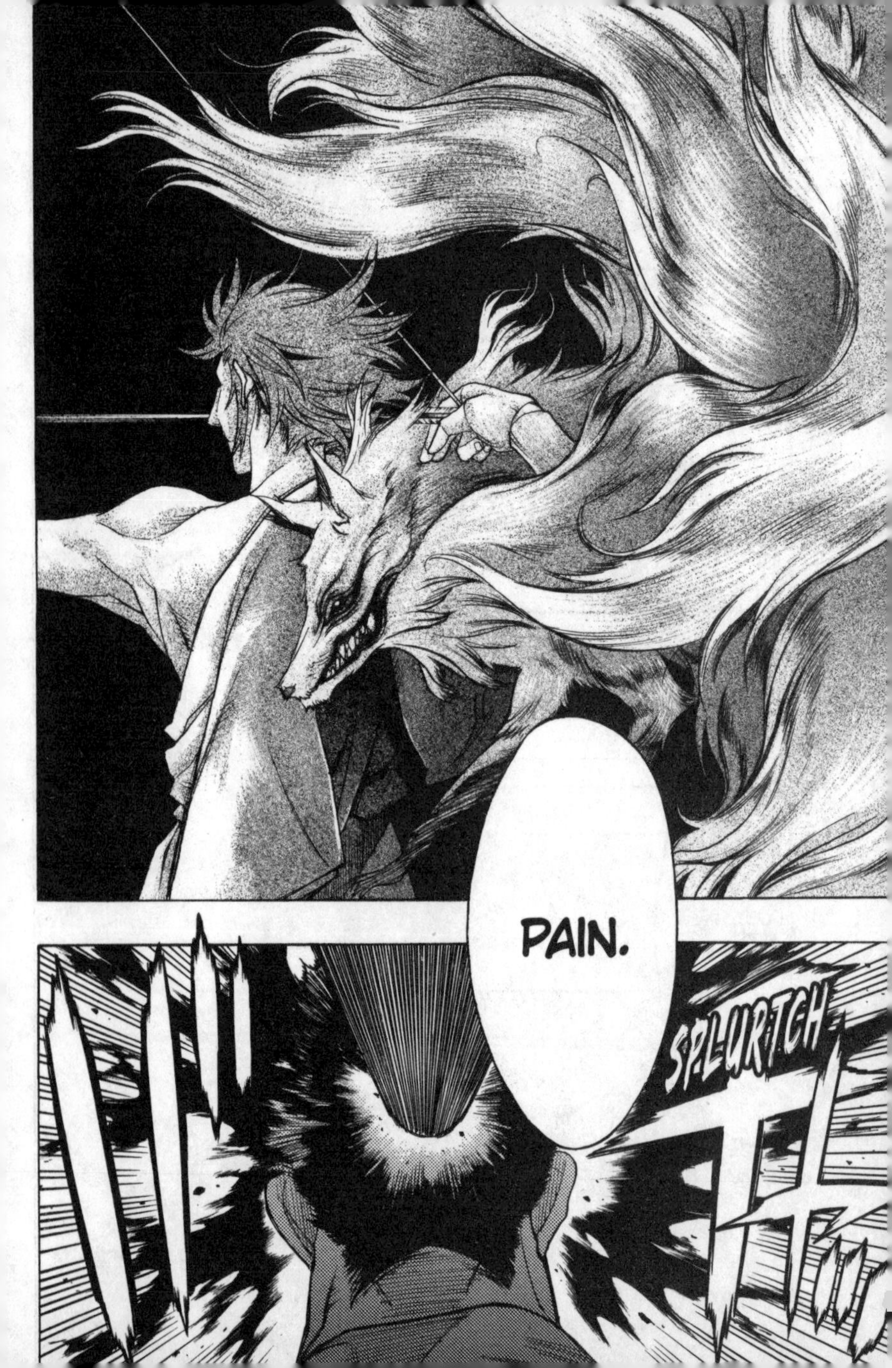
PAIN.
SPLURTCH

HEEEK!
THUD
THOK
THOK

WHAT THE HECK IS THAT?

CHECK IT OUT, BRO.
LOOKS PRETTY BIG, EVEN FROM ALL THE WAY OUT HERE!
IS IT A WALL...? OR MAYBE...A BOARD?

THERE'S NO WAY THERE'D BE A LONE BOARD STANDING IN THE MIDDLE OF NOWHERE. THERE HAS TO BE A REASON FOR IT.
AH!
THERE ARE PEOPLE NEAR IT!

GYAH!

WHAT IS IT, DORORO?
N-NAH, IT'S NOTHIN'... JUST FELT LIKE OUR EYES MET, EVEN OVER ALL THAT DISTANCE.

WAIT A SEC.
DO I *KNOW* THAT PERSON?

IS SOMETHING THE MATTER, TAHOMARU-SAMA?

HEH HEH.

A RAT WAS WATCHING.
IT WAS ONLY FOR AN INSTANT, BUT THEY SHIVERED AND RAN AWAY.
!

SHALL WE TRACK THEM DOWN AND DEAL WITH THEM?
NO NEED. LET THEM GO.

FWEEEE

KA-CLOP
KA-CLOP

I'M GOING TO STOP BY THE DOCTOR'S PLACE TO BE EXAMINED.
THE REST OF YOU STAY HERE AND KEEP UP THE WATCH ON BANMON!
YES, SIR!

HUH...? HE LEFT.
OVER HERE, YOU TWO.

KEEP YOUR HEADS DOWN AND TAKE A LOOK.
THERE'S A RESTLESS SMELL IN THE AIR.

AHA... SO THERE WAS A VILLAGE ON THIS SIDE OF THE HILL?

GOT SOME SAMURAI...
AND...

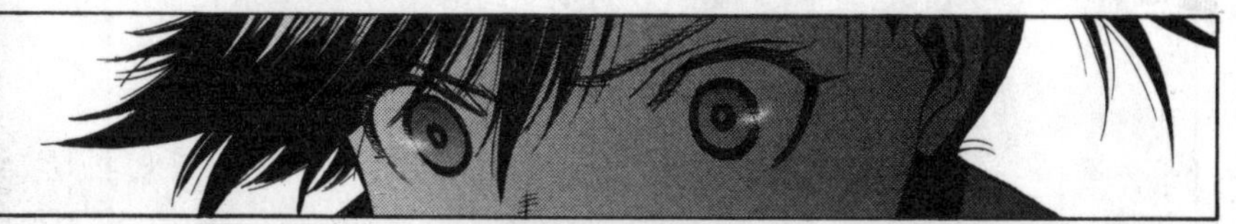

AH!

WHY ARE THOSE PEASANTS LINED UP? WHUH AH AY HOOING?

THEY WOULDN'T... WOULD THEY?

LISTEN UP!

YOU ARE ACCUSED OF ATTEMPTING TO CROSS BANMON AND LEAVE DAIGO TERRITORY!
WAAAAH!
ああん

!!
BANMON!
THERE-FORE, YOU WILL BE EXECUTED IN ACCORDANCE WITH THE LAW!
THE REST OF YOU, TAKE A GOOD, LONG LOOK AT WHAT BECOMES OF THOSE WHO BREAK THE LAW!
WHOOSH
!
HEY! DORORO!!

WAIT, CHILD! STOP!
READY ARROWS!!
LOOSE!!
SHWIP
SHWIP
SHWIP

GYAAAAH!
THUNK
THUNK
ARRGH!
THUNK
ああWAAAH!ん
あWAAAH!ん
......
ああWAAAH!ん

WHAT ARE YOU WAITING FOR?! THERE IS NO EXCEPTION FOR WOMEN AND CHILDREN!
B-BUT, MAKUWA-SAMA...
THEY ARE ALL HEINOUS CRIMINALS WHO HAVE BROKEN THE LAW!
FOOM
FOOM
FOOM

CREAK
SHUMP
SHUMP

THUD
LEAVE THE BODIES AS AN EXAMPLE!
THIS IS WHAT HAPPENS TO ALL WHO BREAK DAIGO-SAMA'S LAW BY TRYING TO CROSS BANMON!
HOLD IT RIGHT THERE!
STOMP
YOU HACK SAMURAI!

HEY, HEY, HEY!!
I DON'T CARE WHAT THIS LAW OF YOURS IS! HOW CAN YOU KILL EVEN WOMEN AND CHILDREN LIKE THEY'RE JUST BUGS?! ARE YOU GUYS EVEN HUMAN?!
GRIN
ギョ
ERK!

TELL ME...
DO YOU DARE DEFY DAIGO-SAMA AS WELL...?

GULP

I DON'T KNOW WHO THIS DAIGO GUY IS...
BUT ANYBODY WHO'D KILL INNOCENT WOMEN AND KIDS IS NO HUMAN!
I ALREADY KNOW HE'S A MONSTER IN HUMAN SKIN!

WHINNY
A MONSTER IN HUMAN SKIN, EH...?

HOW AMUSING.
SNEER

KRAK
M-MAKUWA-SAMA!
TCH!
YOU STUPID SAMURAI!
WAIT AND SEE! I'LL AVENGE THOSE PEASANTS' DEATHS!

UGH...!
THIS LITTLE BRAT...
ALL IN THE LAND WHO DEFY DAIGO-SAMA...
SHINK

WILL BE
PUNISHED!

......!

......
BRO!

I CAN'T LET YOU KILL THIS KID.

ALSO, I HAVE QUESTIONS FOR YOU PEOPLE.

DEMONS... THAT'S WHAT I THOUGHT.
OR... NO... ARE THEY BEING CONTROLLED BY ONE...?

MY BODY ISN'T REACTING TO IT... FOR NOW...

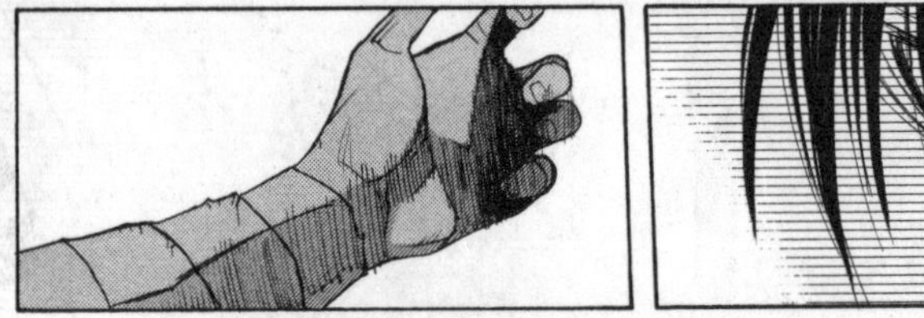

BUT I FEEL IT.

I CAN FEEL IT...!
A DEMON WHO STOLE A PIECE OF MY BODY, IN THIS AREA...!

!

LICK
YOU HAVE A LOT OF NERVE, BRAT.

OH, BUT HOW YOU'VE PIQUED MY INTER-EST...
YIKES!
SHUDDER
KILL ALL WHO DEFY DAIGO-SAMA!
KILL ALL WHO CROSS BAN-MON!
THIS IS THE LAW!!

KILL THOSE WHO BREAK THE LAW!!
DASH
THUNK

SLRSH
ZWRSH

?!
WHOOSH

DO THEY NOT FEEL PAIN...?
THESE GUYS ARE TROUBLE...!!

NO...
IT'S MORE THAN THAT...
WHOOM

MY ATTACKS AREN'T LANDING WHERE I AIM?
MY REACTION TIMES...!
ARE TOO SLOW!!
IS THIS BECAUSE I REGAINED MY REAL EYES...?

UH-
OH...

HUFF!
HUFF!
HUFF!

FOX-
FIRE...

DORO-
RO.
ARE
YOU
HURT?

AH!

DORORO!!
HYA-
KIII-
MA-
RUUU!
KA-CLOP
KA-CLOP
KA-CLOP

BROOOOO!!
DOR
ORO!!

BHRRR!

JUKAI-SENSEI!
ARE YOU THERE?! IT'S ME, TAHOMARU!
OH, TAHOMARU-DONO!

I'M VERY GLAD TO SEE YOU.

どろろと
百鬼丸伝

THE LEGEND OF
DORORO AND HYAKKIMARU

The Legend of Banmon: Part II

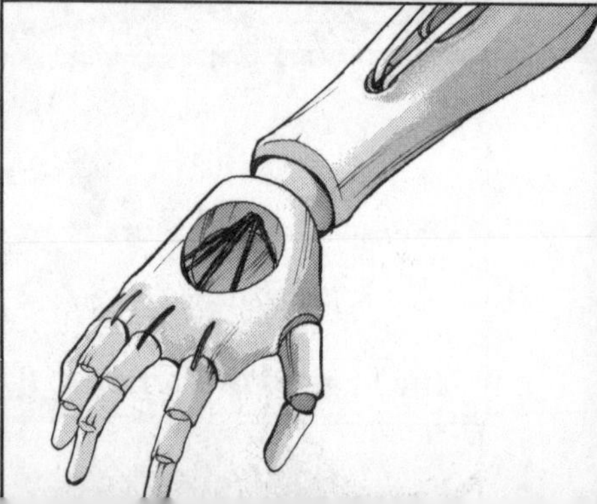

YOU PUSH YOURSELF TOO HARD, TAHOMARU-DONO.

HALF OF YOUR BODY MAY BE OF MY CREATION...

BUT THE OTHER HALF IS YOUR OWN PRECIOUS FLESH AND BLOOD.

TO TAKE AN ARROW AND THEN RIP IT RIGHT OUT? IT IS TOO RECKLESS...

......
ARE YOU SAYING I OUGHTN'T PLACE TOO MUCH TRUST IN THESE PROSTHETICS?

HEH HEH!
FOR TWO YEARS NOW, YOU'VE GIVEN LIFE TO HALF OF MY BODY.
I HAVE COMPLETE CONFIDENCE IN YOU.

SNAP
......

JUKAI-SENSEI.

YOU ONCE TOLD ME OF YOUR SON...
TO WHOM YOU GAVE THIS MECHANICAL BODY.
WAS HE ABLE TO USE HIS BODY BETTER THAN I?

I WONDER...

IT HAS BEEN TWO YEARS AND FOUR MONTHS SINCE MY SON SET OUT ON A JOURNEY...
BY THIS TIME...
I DO NOT KNOW WHERE HE IS, OR EVEN WHAT HIS LIFE IS LIKE.

KOFF!

HACK!
!!
JUKAI-SENSEI!!

D...DO NOT BE CONCERNED.
I SIMPLY HADN'T BRACED MYSELF, BECAUSE I HADN'T HAD A FIT IN SOME TIME...

SENSEI...
HAVE YOU LOST WEIGHT AGAIN...?

HA HA... I AM FINE... JUST FINE.
I CAN'T DIE YET.

NOT BEFORE I SEE MY SON AGAIN...

AH YES... TAHO-MARU-DONO.
TO ANSWER YOUR QUES-TION...

YOU SURPASS HIM, INSOFAR AS **YOU** WERE ABLE TO MOVE YOUR MECHANICAL BODY WITH EASE.

I'M HONORED.

RUSTLE

CAW!
CAW!
CAW!
CAW!

HUFF!
SKRSH
HUFF!

HUFF!

DAMN IT!
HOW MUCH TIME HAS PASSED SINCE I LOST SIGHT OF YOU, DORORO? WHERE WERE YOU TAKEN?

CREAK

IDIOT!

DORORO, YOU COMPLETE IDIOT! WHY WOULD YOU RUSH IN THERE WHEN YOU DIDN'T STAND A CHANCE?!
IS ANYONE THERE?!
TELL ME...
WHERE IS THE LOCAL MAGIS-TRATE'S OFFICE ?!
YOU STILL HAVE BOTH MY ARMS!
......

HEH HEH HEH!
!
THAT DEADLY AURA YOU'RE GIVING OFF WOULD SCARE AWAY ANYBODY BUT DEMONS.

WELL, C'MON INSIDE.
I'LL ASK FOR DIRECTIONS TO THE MAGISTRATE'S OFFICE WITH YA.

FWUP

HA HA!
WELL, LOOK WHAT WE HAVE HERE...

YOU'RE A STRANGE ONE.
WH...

CREAK
WHAT ...?

THOSE ARMS OF YOURS.
THEY'LL SCARE PEOPLE AWAY EVEN WORSE THAN YOUR SHOUTING.

SHRIP

MASTER! GONNA BORROW YOUR CURTAIN!
AND BRING THIS FELLOW SOME SAKE!
EEP! A- ALL YERS!

AT LEAST WRAP THIS AROUND THEM TO DAMPEN THAT DANGEROUS AURA.

I DON'T DRINK.
YOU HEARD HIM! MAKE THAT ONE CUP OF TEA!!

THE MAGISTRATE'S OFFICE YOU WERE HOWLING ABOUT...
IF YOU MEAN THE LOCAL MILITARY GOVERNOR, METHINKS YOU'RE LOOKING FOR THE MANOR OF DAIGO'S SON. THE FELLOW WHO CONTROLS BANMON.

BANMON AGAIN...
MASTER! DRAW THIS YOUNG SAMURAI A MAP TO THE MANOR!
R...
RIGHT AWAY!

HEY.

WHAT IS BANMON?
!!

YOU DON'T KNOW?
YOU'RE SOME-THING ELSE... I TAKE IT YOU AREN'T FROM AROUND HERE, THEN.
ALL RIGHT, FINE.

I'M IN A GOOD MOOD RIGHT NOW.
WHILE WE WAIT ON THE MASTER OF THIS FINE ESTABLISHMENT, I S'POSE I'LL TELL YOU A TALE.
THE STORY BEHIND BANMON...

IT BEGAN FIFTEEN OR SIXTEEN YEARS AGO. THE TOGASHI CLAN, WHO HAD BEEN FIGHTING OVER THIS TERRITORY'S BORDER...
BURNED DOWN THE PEASANT HOUSES ON THE FRINGES AND BUILT AN EXTRAORDINARILY TALL WALL TO ENFORCE IT. THAT'S BANMON.

THIS LAND HAS AN ABUNDANCE OF MINABLE ORES...
SO THE TERRITORIAL DISPUTES ARE FIERCE, YOU SEE.

ONCE BANMON WAS BUILT, CROSSING THE BOR-DER WAS EXPRESSLY FORBIDDEN.
THE BAN HELD EVEN IF YOU HAD RELATIVES--EVEN YOUR OWN MOTHER--LIVING ON THE OTHER SIDE.

AFTER THAT, THE TOGASHI CLAN WAS **REPLACED** BY THE **DAIGO CLAN**, THEIR VASSALS WHO HAD GROWN IN STRENGTH.
BUT **BANMON** REMAINED.
SEVERAL WARS ON THE BORDER CAME AND WENT.

MOST OF BANMON BURNED DOWN. NOW ONLY A SMALL POR- TION OF IT STILL STANDS.
FOR THE LOCALS, THOUGH, AN UNSEEN WALL STILL LOOMS.
A WALL CALLED **THE LAW.**

SO THAT'S THE NATURE...
OF BANMON!

I-IT'S DONE.
GREAT!

LOOKS GOOD.
NICE AND EASY TO UNDER-STAND.
PHEW!
THANKS FOR YOUR TIME, MASTER.

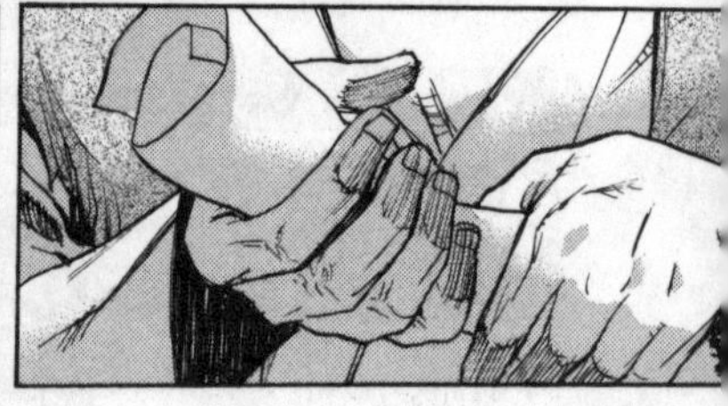

SMILE

I...
SHOULD REPAY YOU...

AH, THERE'S NO NEED FOR THAT.
LIKE I TOLD YOU, I'M IN A GOOD MOOD AT THE MOMENT.

WELL, TO BE PRECISE...
IT'S NOT **ME** AS SUCH.

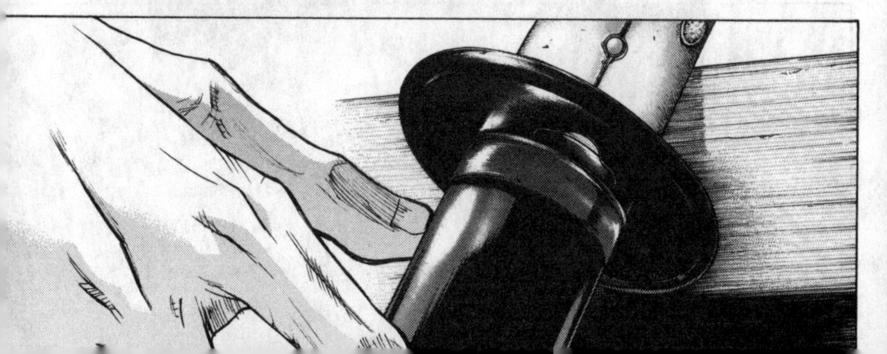

NIHIL HERE HAS A FULL BELLY AND IS IN A SPLENDID MOOD FOR THE MOMENT.
SHUDDER

THROB
THROB
THIS MAN, HE'S...!
THROB
CLINK
THROB
......
CLATTER
YOUR NAME...

AH-AH... IT'S BEST FOR BOTH OF US NOT TO GIVE OUR NAMES.
OUR PATHS WILL CROSS AGAIN, IF THAT'S WHAT FATE HAS IN STORE FOR US.

WHAT ARE YOU STANDING THERE FOR? AREN'T YOU IN A HURRY?
GO ON, GET OUT OF HERE.

THAT SWORD... IS IT POSSESSED BY A DEMON...?
IT HAS A DIFFERENT PRESENCE THAN THE ONE I FELT WHEN I FOUGHT THOSE SOLDIERS...

NO...

RIGHT NOW, DORORO COMES FIRST...!

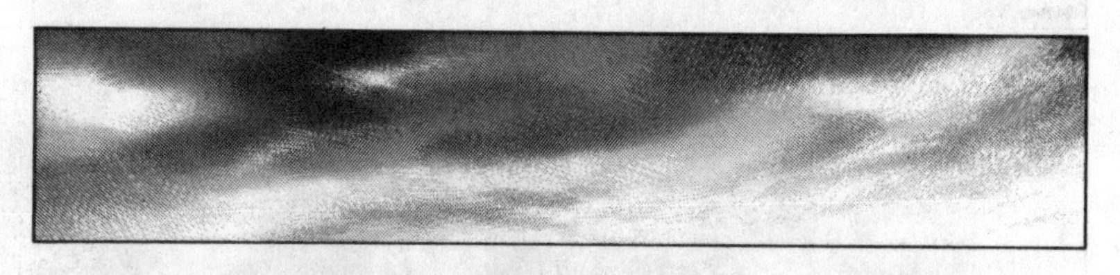

バタン
WHUMP
ドタ
THUNK

ARE YOU CRAZY?!
THUNK
STAY AWAY FROM ME, YOU DIMWIT!
BAM

WHAT'S ALL THAT NOISE?

IT'S MAKUWA-SAMA'S VICE.
OH GREAT... HE'S GOT ANOTHER KID...?

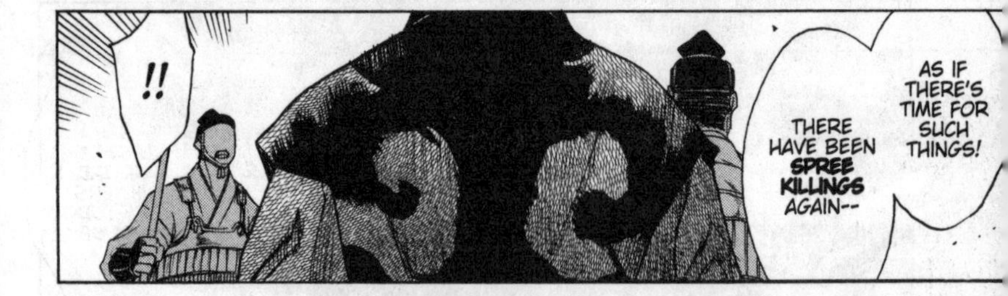
AS IF THERE'S TIME FOR SUCH THINGS!
THERE HAVE BEEN **SPREE KILLINGS** AGAIN--
!!

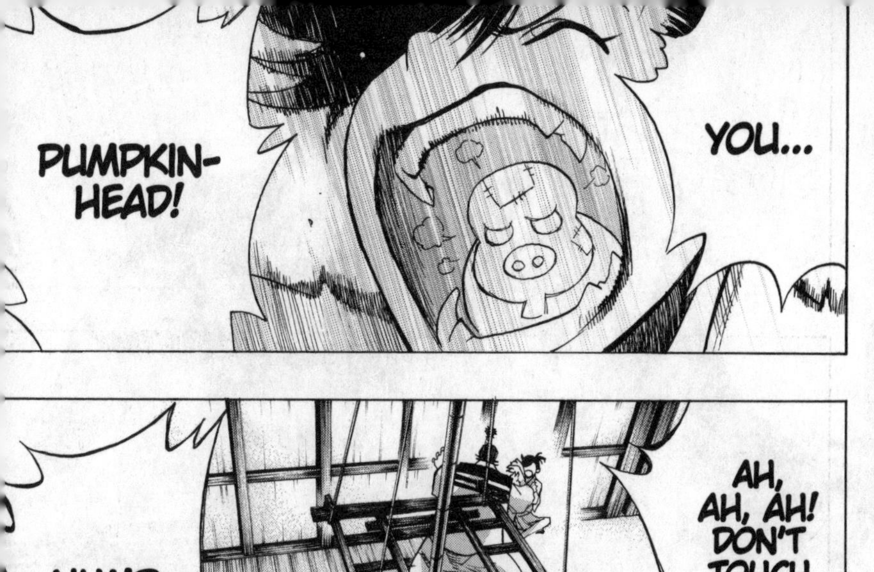
YOU...
PUMPKIN-HEAD!

AH, AH, AH! DON'T TOUCH ME!
NUMB-SKULL!

GOOD, VERY GOOD! I LIKE THE FIGHTERS LIKE YOU BEST OF ALL.
GO ON! BETTER RUN AWAY, OR I'LL GET YOU!
SCREW YOU, YOU DAMN PERVERT ...!

!

GRIP

HUH ?!
AH!
T...
TAHO-MARU-SAMA?!
AH...
AH...!
I-I CAN EX-PLAIN!
AAAAH!

AAARGH!!
SPLR
AAAAAA
RRR
SHH
AAA
AAAA
FRRRSHHHHH
AAAA
AAA
AAA
AHH!

H... H...
HAVE... MER... CY...
THWAM
THWAM
SPLURTCH
SPLATCH
SPLURSH
YEEEEK!
SPLURCH

ぐちゃ
THWAM
WH... WHAT'S GOING ON...?
ACTUALLY, WHO CARES? THIS IS MY CHANCE TO ESCAPE...
Y...
YOU...

YOU'RE...
THAT SAMURAI...
IT'S YOU! FROM THE FOG...!

——!!
THOSE ARMS...!!
To be continued...

どろろと
百鬼丸伝

THE LEGEND OF
DORORO AND HYAKKIMARU

HUFF!

HUFF!

HUFF!

On the village out-skirts, you'll come upon a pond. Beyond it, there'll be a river split into two branches.
From there, just follow the map and you'll find your way to--

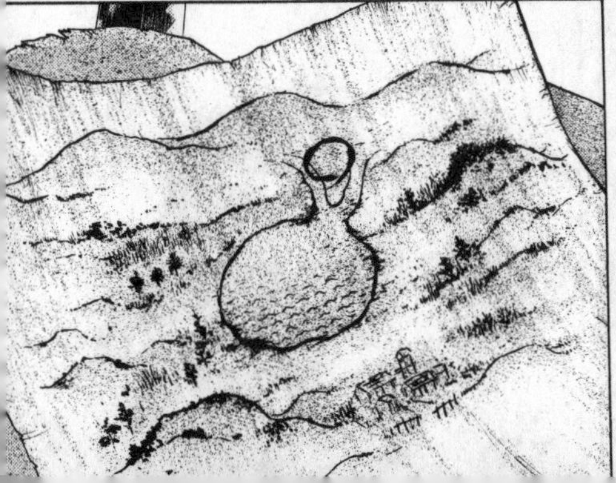

WHAT THE HELL?!
WHERE'S THIS TWO-BRANCHED RIVER? WHERE AM I RIGHT NOW IN THE FIRST PLACE?

HYEE HEE...

YOU'VE A KEEN NOSE FOR **DANGER,** BUT NO HEAD FOR **DIRECTIONS,** IT SEEMS.
OLD MAN...!

WHERE THE HELL HAVE YOU BEEN?!
HYEE HEE HEE!
WHY SO UPSET?
DON'T TELL ME YOU NEEDED HELP FROM THIS BLIND OLD MAN?

WHAT?!
HYEE HEE!

I AM ONLY WATCHING OVER **YOUR** FATE.

DO YOU NOT CARE WHAT HAPPENS TO DORORO?

IT'S NOT MY JOB TO CLEAN UP YOUR MISTAKES.

COME, LET'S TAKE A LITTLE WALK AND FIND YOUR RIVER.

TELL ME...
HYAKKI-MARU.

YOU DON'T SEEM TO UNDER-STAND *WHY* DORORO RUSHED INTO THAT HOPELESS SITUATION.
BUT YOU MUSTN'T EXPECT TO UNDER-STAND ANOTHER PERSON EASILY.
AS SOMEONE WHO'S TRAVELED **ALONE** UNTIL NOW, IT MAY BE DIFFICULT FOR YOU, BUT...

YOU'RE BEING TAUGHT...
WHAT IT MEANS TO LIVE WITH COMPANIONSHIP BY DORORO, DON'T YOU THINK?

YOU REALLY THINK...
I'M LEARNING THINGS... FROM *DORORO?*

TRICKLE
LISTEN.
YOU CAN HEAR TWO CURRENTS OVER YONDER.
TRICKLE
MAYHAP THAT'S THE SPLIT RIVER FROM YOUR MAP?
GO TAKE A LOOK. OUGHT TO BE A DWELLING THERE.

THE MAGIS-TRATE'S OFFICE IS ON THE OTHER SIDE...!
TMP

SO VERY FRANTIC...

METHINKS FIGHTING TOOTH AND NAIL TO HELP **SOMEONE ELSE...**
MORE CLOSELY RESEMBLES YOUR TRUE NATURE, HYAKKIMARU.

Hyakkimaru and Tahomaru. Two young men with mechanical bodies.
and Hyakkimaru, Volume 3!!

At last, their paths collide!
Don't miss *The Legend of Dororo*

SEVEN SEAS ENTERTAINMENT PRESENTS

THE LEGEND OF DORORO AND HYAKKIMARU

VOLUME 2

story and art by SATOSHI SHIKI original story by OSAMU TEZUKA

TRANSLATION
Amanda Haley

LETTERING AND RETOUCH
Meaghan Tucker

INTERIOR LAYOUT
Christa Meisner

COVER DESIGN
Nicky Lim
(LOGO) Kris Aubin

PROOFREADER
Brett Hallahan

EDITOR
J.P. Sullivan

PREPRESS TECHNICIAN
Rhiannon Rasmussen-Silverstein

PRODUCTION MANAGER
Lissa Pattillo

MANAGING EDITOR
Julie Davis

ASSOCIATE PUBLISHER
Adam Arnold

PUBLISHER
Jason DeAngelis

Seven Seas press and purchase enquiries can be sent to Marketing Manager Lianne Sentar at press@gomanga.com. Information regarding the distribution and purchase of digital editions is available from Digital Manager CK Russell at digital@gomanga.com.

ISBN: 978-1-64505-760-4

Printed in Canada

First Printing: October 2020

10 9 8 7 6 5 4 3 2 1

FOLLOW US ONLINE: ***www.sevenseasentertainment.com***

READING DIRECTIONS

This book reads from ***right to left***, Japanese style. If this is your first time reading manga, you start reading from the top right panel on each page and take it from there. If you get lost, just follow the numbered diagram here. It may seem backwards at first, but you'll get the hang of it! Have fun!!

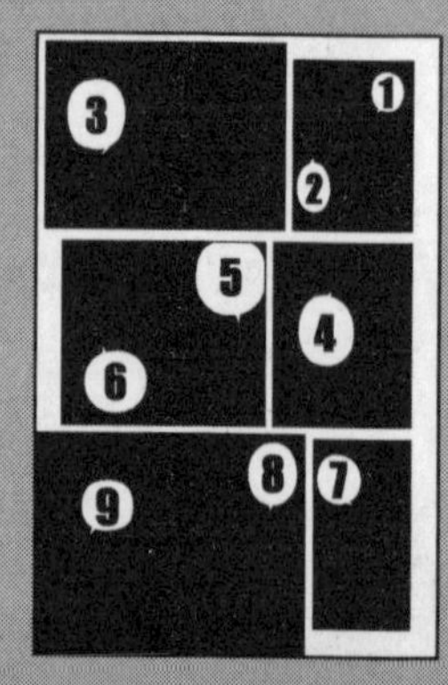